More praise for *There Is Only the Sacred and the Desecrated*

Steeped in Rilke, attuned to Whitman, Mary Buchinger has written a Book of Hours chronicling moments that mesh the physical with the spiritual. Her openness to the world causes worlds to open within her. She penetrates the growth of a tree in good years and hard years by reading the formation of its rings as readily as she reaches into the life of Francis of Assisi, illuminating his understanding of the sacred, his ailments, and his love for and ministering to animals as well as people. We, her readers, partake of the joy that arises from her encounters with what she sees and feels. And when she pulls aside a curtain to show us a scene remembered from many years earlier, lodged next to the "left ventricle" of her heart, we learn the heart of the matter: art thrives on conjuring the real.

— Jennifer Barber, author of *The Sliding Boat Our Bodies Made*

There Is Only the Sacred and the Desecrated

Mary Buchinger

LILY POETRY REVIEW BOOKS

Copyright © 2026 by Mary Buchinger

All rights reserved. Published in the United States by Lily Poetry Review Books.

Library of Congress Control Number: 2025944143

Cover design and Layout: Michael McInnis
Cover image: "Seville" by Kai Bodwell
Author photo: Stephen Bodwell

ISBN: 978-1-957755-69-4

Published by Lily Poetry Review Books
223 Winter Street
Whitman, MA 02382
lilypoetryreview.blog/

In memory of Fanny Howe

What I trusted as a child, I now believe.

~

What do you like about Christianity? I mean, what is it?

A beauty-filled vision of reality where there is a quiet that creates a resting place between the one who sees and the one who is seen. The space, called the spirit, is self-contained and keeps braiding itself into lines, dimensions, circles that cross each other and meet and move on while its wind (or Word) whirls with it, and produces thought, and thought produces speech, all of it contributing to the speed of evolution. So every word comes into existence as a sound, then slides back into non-existence. People get depressed by all this coming and going. They grow ill, weak, they die but the mystery survives.

Contents

Seeds

Germination	4
uttering joyous leaves all its life	5
What the trees see to	6
The Interview	8
In the bin of what I'm looking for –	9
I lean my body	10
At the Cemetery	11
Unbound	12
On my way to work	15
And the engines play on	16
Birth of Night	17

Orbits

Parable of the Moss Piglet	22
Once a molecule said	23
Lodged beside my left ventricle a little village on a blue volcano ringed with red clay paths	26
In the Park	28
A Broken Sonnet for the Sparrow Trapped in the Interfaith Center on the 3rd Floor of the McCormick Building at UMass Boston Overlooking the Harbor	30
The Border Patrol Agent	31
Bare ruin'd choirs –	32
from the world of things a feeling	34
You can read it in its rings	35
To the Raven Feeding on Carrion on the Side of the Road	36

Parable of the Krill	37
Harold calls to me	39
Waiting	40
how readily I assign holy	42

Hours

Canoeing at Dusk	45
Late October Leaves	48
Now when darkness starts in midafternoon	49
In the Company of Grief	50
Sometimes Necessity	52
Translating Edip Cansever's poem with my friend Adnan Adam Onart	53
The first story of the snow	54
Lincoln's Throat	55
Moon Bird Tree	56
The day my father died	58
Demolition of the Old Hotel	61
The year is new again	63

The Sacred

Prefigure	66
Theory of Everything	67
Spring, and	69
Spring upspring	70
There is only the sacred and the desecrated	71
Song	85
Notes and Acknowledgments	86
Author Bio	90

There Is Only the Sacred and the Desecrated

I know that nothing has ever been real
without my beholding it.
All becoming has needed me.
My looking ripens things
and they come toward me, to meet and be met.

                        Rainer Maria Rilke, *Book of Hours*

Seeds

Listen – don't you hear something?
Aren't there voices other than mine?

                    Rainer Maria Rilke, *Book of Hours*

Germination

it isn't a choice
the sluice opens
the little seed shakes
it breathes hurts
shudders and swells
something gives
and it becomes
what it's never
been before

uttering joyous leaves all its life
 — *Walt Whitman*

I greet the ancient flowering cherry
  on the green bank of the fens

   this tree gnarly narrow-waisted
  speckled with deer moss
leans toward my path

  its brittle branches
bear torches of blossoms
that stand in air making sun bend
(messenger whispering
in the many ears)

      in its trunk a hole
     broader than any
       of its living parts

I kneel and slip my arm
hand wrist elbow through
     the wide cleft
  edges round with mending
I wave to the other side

What the trees see to

We bring to the trees whatever it is we live in

Mine is crisp chevy-blue with hot yellow seats
    chock-full of animals
        some are memories of animals
        companions I hold into the night

   It takes me from here to there
holds everything I subsist on
                it's /recognizable/
Oh, that is your life they say   Well, I reply,
   This is my life /today/

        Hard-shelled
traveling grenade   protects and promises
  some day
     to explode

        I thought it was a helmet
my friend says knocking on my trunk
  my ladybug my green splintered bone

        It grew overnight I tell her
  my skin has always been
/unpredictable/ like that

In fact, it's the earth's crust and it's over my head
    my meconium, its cambium   the conversion of light
    to sugar   the shingled hood   a lovely leafy roof

hands nails my braid of breakable plates
          books couches rugs pixels bran
     and held dear /within/ the many cats
          three dogs   one leaping Guernsey calf

I drive all of it to the forest
  Please, I say, look me over,
        employ your /implements/

The Interview

Massachusetts Avenue: *Where is your wheel? Your bike-body?*
Sturdy-car-self?
Woman: *My bags are heavy. My hat is warm. Do you speak French?*

Dream: *That child in your arms, his eager weight, can you protect him?*
Self: *Are those falling stars in the night sky, or deadly tracers?*

Open Bottle of Beer On the Grave: *Will I shatter on the granite marker, be drunk by the fresh-dug mouth of earth?*
Young Men: *Effervesce like a joke with a scorpion tail*

Time: *What can I do to you?*
Yew: *My crown may become irregular, my sex may change, still the thrush will love me*

Air: *Which of my weaves pleases you most?*
Hawk: *Pockets, please, for me to hang inside. May I rip your seam and glide?*

Paper: *What shape – what curved dotted stand-up mark – shall be impressed upon my field?*
Pencil: *A scritch, a scratch, a residue. How could I be anything, let alone, enough?*

In the bin of what I'm looking for —

the what of ecstasy and half of how

a long line of winter trees at the edge
of a winter field   the word for that

　　the velvet a drake must feel
beneath his neat-pleated wing

December's hawk: a clot
　on the crown of a sky-etched oak

I lift up the river beside me peer
into its deepest eye

　　　　　how naked it is
summer asleep somewhere inside

I lean my body

   against the single
bone-straight Tree

test it with my weight
Are you alive?

My neck bends backward
cartilage against cartilage
throat to the sky

I do not understand Tree
Tree does not understand me
Are you alive? it asks and asks

At the Cemetery

In the greeny dell below me
a man gestures talking loud
I'm telling you

a glowing congregation
of white headstones
surrounds him

    some lean half-sunk
others wrangled by tree roots
 ropes of ivy grip stone roses

clouds bat the sun
    as the last of summer's bees
        reap late blue flowers

How alive his dead
gathered round him
      listening

Unbound

i.

    a grey-blue shadow
draws my eye into a succession
of masses piled
in the sky
            each cloud
bears its relation to light
and to others

      I watch a wisp of cirrus
tuck behind the many-storied
Prudential

     seagulls   windows   cars
street meters   scatter the sun

    a skyscraper ripples
on the river
        and I see Whitman's
fine centrifugal spokes of light
round the shape of my head
in the sunlit water

           loose ends
make the whole
whole

ii.

                a path leads me
through the fens' untidy
banks of reeds
              where red-winged
blackbirds scold and wobble
on tawny stalks
          seeds take flight

iii.

      Yesterday I held
a mourning brooch
that Fanny Longfellow
once pinned to her dress

      a ring of broken black
onyx surrounds its glass
oval window

      and curled inside
is a lock of brown hair
  from the head of Henry's
    sister   dead at twenty

iv.

        I stop to watch
a golden retriever race
     through an open field
of late winter snow

      the dog in morning sun
is a bundle of riotous ends

bounding with a cache
       of light – its own
         spoked halo

On my way to work

I watch a hawk at the edge
of a muddy puddle drink
the way birds do:

beak dips head stretches up
the liquid traveling down
the extended throat

The pooled water gives of itself
unlike the hawk's rabbit yesterday
which had to be gripped hard

to be unpacked the furred
skirt of the gut pinned down
the bloodied beak pecking

and pulling hook and talons
toiling in tandem
to dismember the meal

And the engines play on

motors trawl tympani air and all the leaves of all the trees applaud the saw the teeth the gear the sky *oh my!* they tumble me   tumble me down *Come St. Catherine! Come!* wheel round 'n round   cart 'n dance – the heart   full-fueled the start 'n clink   just flip a switch and the human shall speak or bite or build a church or cast a stone – a cornerstone! and raise an army of moths of mass deconstruction   So take my kettle of bone and restless blood down   to the green trestletree forest to the takeaway river no pestle no mortar no *life is but*   no *row-row-row* just roses of Sharon   in the pipe of Charon the   sweet-thick smoke   a streaming   machine say yes yes *yes* to the lovely oily rainbowy   sheen

Birth of Night

I watched in my sleep
   the moon crowning
      the vaginal horizon

    earth and sky together
       bore down
     and the light was both
   new and ancient

.

When I see a photo in the news
  of a black hole (nothing light within)
   caught mid-swallow
    devouring a sun-size star (the star
 unraveling gold   gone raggedy
in the perfection of gravity's mouth)
   I remember my dream of round

. .

Walking with my dog
in the city park the roundness
of a large mown hill swells beside me

all along its curved edge human silhouettes
(unmoored stars) move against the sky
first one and then another   strangers
having nothing to do with me or each other
bound only by the round

. . .

High tide at Carson Beach
    I float beside a flotilla
of migrating geese the half-worlds
  of their bodies bob black and white

        I imagine their webbed feet
  balancing on my legs and torso
      how little room they take
(wings-tucked) they paddle
  beside each other   perpetual
movement within the moving ocean

The geese bide their time waiting
  for me   my single splashing body
      (*Swallow her, O Sea*
  is one thing they say)

  and when I re-cognize myself
as obstacle   I unsubmerge my slow
ruminating self take my place
  on the darkening sand

    and they sweep over immediate
the buoyant tide of them gliding
    I watch their long vee
  cross my path in the water

    . . . .

  What is it to be this thing that floats
emerging from fire   parting ocean from sky

 At the end of my seeing the very edge
of what is and what is possible sometimes
 rises half-circle half-being into whole

Orbits

As it happens, the wall between us
is very thin.

> Rainer Maria Rilke, *Book of Hours*

Parable of the Moss Piglet

I am what can happen
when most reduced

jaws and claws
pigment-cup eyes

I'm shaped like a barrel
and move like a bear

my tubular mouth
a sucking pharynx

armed with stylets
I stab the everything I eat

indomitable I thrive
in ice   in fire

when very dry I vitrify
call me *space bear water bear*

I bear it all orbiting earth
or stuck to a paw

I make the way
for predators and prey

five extinctions I've survived
a gray nearly nothing but alive

Once a molecule said

not stone not fish
   not seaweed

what was it that it said
yes to?

   Who was asking?

I just want to know.

   *

I feel my molecules
as predetermined
and choiceless

yet there is wander and drift

there is the body of me
that is fully formed and
fixed

   the body of me
that moves that changes
and is dying.

    *

A ripple of light
  warmed by spring sun
washes over my page

    says *This life is moving*
  moving light

each hour lifts
    the day from night

    from the shadow
      of the known

its warmed current
  rushing rushing –

    *

What is so far
from here
    is still
here
  is shaping here

  the maker of here
the way-way back

the begetter
      that wayward
         Atom.

    *

One day the molecule
        was *not stone*
not fish not seaweed

    no   it was
  more than a day

      it was more
than one thing

     until it was
something

  and then
something new

again.

Lodged beside my left ventricle a little village on a blue volcano ringed with red clay paths

I sit in a plaza
with a friend
who's wearing
a black felt
bowler hat
  my wool cape
clasped with
a wrought
iron breastpin
that could kill
someone
  the table
wobbles
on the dirt
floor (the earth
has never been
perfectly
round
not even
within)
  and though
I am young
in that village
I know I
have to say

goodbye
to my friend
to this moment
at the table
 and (*oh*)
to the beautiful
volcano
– its terrible
fire
fastened
inside

In the Park

*Three elements make
a space into a place:
  a feeling of safety,
  a sense of purpose,
  and a view*
    my son explains
as we swing together
on a wooden bench
suspended from chains
in a city park
far from our home

The view unfolds:
a photographer at work
snapping portraits of a woman
who poses in a purple skirt
beside a matching patch
of royal purple irises

children with lime-green
sno-ball lips
playing on the lawn

  But there is a fourth thing
    he can't remember what

  The model has changed into
a scarlet dress matching satchel

a living wall of ivy pops her red
    she flips her hair
    for the camera

    A woman in fuzzy slippers
stops by our swing
    Oh, I always loved
traveling with my mother! She'd be so
embarrassed if she saw me out here
not wearing proper shoes.

Do you know, I have three hundred gallons
of honey, my husband keeps bees

    We smile for her
Her vape pen clatters
to the sidewalk and falls apart

    She picks up the pieces
then wanders off leaving behind
her insulated mug

    My son rushes to return it to her
    Oh! Thank you! Thank you, sweetheart!

A Broken Sonnet for the Sparrow Trapped in the Interfaith Center on the 3rd Floor of the McCormick Building at UMass Boston Overlooking the Harbor

You dart   flit   no –   this is not   flying
you test   what is   here   the what   *this*
inside this room   that's holding   you and me   up
and   in   yet you   spread your wings   and rise
try   the spin   the span of   this   closed space –
I won't say   *metaphor*   you are you   singular bird
flailing in the Interfaith Center   where "All
Are Welcome"   Beyond us   the sky   we both seek
holds an impenetrable city   on   its   tattered lip
while   the ebbing harbor   abandons   its banks
catching in its blue   littered mirror   the passage
of a stiff-winged airplane – its stolid   steady   flight

The Border Patrol Agent

"We've taken [the children], we've put them into a shelter, given them food, clothing, put them in a climate-controlled environment, and we are protecting them, and then we are processing them as expeditiously and humanely as possible. I would challenge anyone to explain to me how that is immoral." — Terrence Shiggs, veteran border agent

But everywhere I go
I hear them see them
they follow me home and
when I sleep they come –
wrapped in foil blankets
new white tennis shoes
washed faces clean nails
brown eyes long wet lashes
Mamá they cry *Mamá*
spinning intricate webs
luminescent glowing they
surround me catching me
I am turned and turned
in their silky silver foil
I am not hungry not thirsty
I am safe inside a shiny
cold cocoon I am alone

Bare ruin'd choirs —

      Last night
I walked
  past my dead

   friend's house
my feet plowed
  the fallen

leaves beneath
  the borer-ridden
    street ash

words so
  many words
he and I had

   dared to try
out against
  indifferent air —

  Once in a country
I'd never known
  he took my hand

    we crossed
the broken threshold
  of an old chapel

   laced with thistles
crows perched
  on crumbling pews

    the open loft
above us then
  there –

   an absolute
  unburdened
    blue

from the world of things a feeling

last year's leaf litter caught
(by what thread?)
between wind-worn planks
on a sun-bowed deck
built beside a tidal cove

it and I above
the runneled mud
of low tide
shag of seaweed
combed by currents

the small bit of leaf
twists in morning's
breath catches every
gold of light

You can read it in its rings

The tree went through years
of painful amplitude of squeeze and swell
of *do-not-burst* years of formal and copious splendor
of laying down layers of cellulose and burl sucking up
the radiance waving sun-drunk branches high above its head
years of sloppy abundance and running riot years of sleek
and silk of plush and thundering of shadows rising a year
of hard cold rain of *Screw this* a year of *Oh yeah Tell it
to your mama* of *I can not do this any more* of *Take me
hurricane Take me fire* and another year of ringing round
any way gnawed by deer burrowing badgers another year
beetles beetling frost rain sun's soft embrace rays
extending down reaching deep another year mites
mushrooms *Come* every forgiving fungi insect
moss mold *Come* *Come*

To the Raven Feeding on Carrion on the Side of the Road

I too know that needling
   the getting deep inside
   and rummaging
   rooting around
the revelation of delicacies
small explosions of rot

and the need to pause
   see what's yet to be won
   even as the laden table waits

Parable of the Krill

    light and
motion we
Euphausia
are a we
many-
membered
wave upon
wave we
migrate
down we
dune deep
in day up-
welling
swarm we shoal
crest to feast
we sieve
waters sink
full-belly
surge as one
we grow
large and
small down
we spawn
brood broad
flow ocean
through poles
ice weaving

weather we
current the
earth light-
lensed glow-
ing we
shear night
feed shallows
beaming viands
baleen-combed
we die we live
inside the *we*

Harold calls to me

    against the morning slush of February
on my way to the train underground
Spring! he says *Comin' this weekend! Ima gonna
grab hold! Not lettin' go when I grab holda spring!*

Harold and I age-mates greet morning
after morning after morning the we
we are – braid of rope between us
we lumber across tentative into

some inter-middle-ness of self
arising from self and other
never the same wandering
the tension inside the space is

where we live unknowing we music
half-note here and half-note there
melody moving into me-you
where other and other is neither –

    How then to hallow that place
make sacred the self that meets
Harold each morning (if not-Harold
then not-morning for me) I

descending stairs and he *Spare
Change News* in hand waiting below
for hello   and dollars
in air   between us

Waiting

I grow old
on this corner

the trees stark
inert   the empty
street salt white

Somewhere in the city
a car – forest green
Ford and a man
his hands on the wheel

Have I looked
for anyone as long
and as steadily?
The car more familiar
than even myself –

I lean on the cold
metal rod of a Stop
sign   feet planted
on concrete   museum
greenhouse at my back

What if another
man were in the car
today – some other
lover from a different

time   grown bald
and nearsighted looking
for me   would I climb
into that beige interior?
Would my lips
brush that man's too
before the car blinks
left and turns?

how readily I assign holy

slow to rise from soft flannel sheets my skin
receiving taking in fleecy cotton   against
toes ankle calf arm the feeling of being
inside swathed in warmth coffee's aroma
wafting from the kitchen   my dog Dover
nudges open the door   jumps on the bed
settles on top of the quilt her warm weight
against my feet she grooms her   paws
a ritual of cleaning after her breakfast
the movement of her labor is a syncopated
pressure I listen to the sound of her lapping
tongue teeth grazing against something
the changes in her breath as she works
cleaning her toes attending to calloused
pads worn nails her body curled mouth
to paw   her sensitive nuzzle   the soft
of nothing else   what is it about mouths
how vulnerable the places   of the body
that   take in   feeling   punishingly
luxuriously aware   the tender receptors
on which the rest of a life depends
essential sensing guardians and
this body of mine that wishes to stay here
beside Dover within this winter morning hour

Hours

Nearby is the country they call life.
You will know it by its seriousness.

Give me your hand.

                    Rainer Maria Rilke, *Book of Hours*

Canoeing at Dusk

One hermit thrush
and then another

tosses silver floss
back and forth

breaks and binds
the green forest

shears minute
from hour

   o

   In the sparse top
of the tallest spruce
the lump of an eagle
unbundles its feathers
hoists its thick body up
in sky over us

      and over the loons
   who suspend their hunting

   Remember!
they cry crazily
Remember!

   their warbled marble calls
     tumble across the glass
       plate of still water

  o

Two girls in two
orange kayaks call
Do you hear me?

Do you? You?
Hear me? Me?

the ring of granite
rings back

  o

I turn to you
   our paddles lifted
   as we listen

to the eerie
trebling
of voices

Whatever we say
to each other
in this place

    will linger
   between us
long after dark

Late October Leaves

The first one I
pick up (gold
and tarnished copper)
is dead and changing
still, its veins –
avenues of green
life ripening
into death

More leaves call
and I collect
them one by
one, each a
separate body
of work a harvest
of summer light
and air

Now when darkness starts in midafternoon
— *Eavan Boland*

I tend my inner
daisies, hands stained
with clay, I consider
my origins, my
first firstness

how the air was
neither dark nor
light in that moment
of beginning

sure it was
already closing
like a December
day, the winter
tucked inside

the ova too
ready to unfold
like heliotrope
and pine

the hour – infant
day, seated seed
to petal out
its rounds of gold

In the Company of Grief

1.

One day I decide
I will teach Grief to talk

Grief wants to learn
the most expensive words
I pretend I don't know them

but Grief persists
   rummages through my pockets
   unclenches my hands
   raids my bank

and they spill out
each precious coin

2.

I take Grief for a walk
fresh air stretch the legs
naturally we get lost

at first everything is familiar
we've been here before
just like this hand in hand

but it grows dark and I don't
remember where we turned
how far we've walked

the houses are vacant
curtains pulled shut
no one to ask directions

3.

Grief tells me
it wants to be a flower

Okay, I say, and hand Grief
over to a cup of dried-up
daffodils, petals splay
like flung coats
    the misshapen mouths
      collapse on themselves

Grief climbs into the crisp
fringes of concentrated gold
and settles into the papery spathes

    sprung-open ladles empty
  no – filled with all that is not

Sometimes Necessity

       sets the table

          hour hungering
    after hour

something in us eats itself
         against the cold

night's window cradles
      a hammock moon

        a scatter
    of ungatherable stars

  Let crumbs reconstruct a loaf

        we'll keep
   what can be kept
uncounted –

        the candle
whittled
    by draft and fire

  I will not parse our love

Translating Edip Cansever's poem with my friend Adnan Adam Onart

   the description of a young lover
standing at the train station
ticket window on the last
day of November stirs me

   she is alone, money
in her hand and I
tell you, I don't
want to sell her
the ticket, she must not
leave, not like that –

I can't believe this
is how it ends

The first story of the snow

   is the snow

      its flecked silver
tenting
   then tent

  what the wind said
to the dry tussock
sedge   lisp of meadow
rue inscribed

   mouse mutterings slight
beside the stamp of deer

     rambling animal sentences
feel their way
between the trees

  and leap the path
by the thin-iced
stream   where

    on the bank
  a tamped-down
    plot–

       small pink bed
cold violence –

  another passage
     told in snow

Lincoln's Throat

a ravine on Mt. Lincoln, White Mountains, New Hampshire

It began when all was very cold
                                      scraped by a heavy moving slowness
its weight turned mobile
                                      as warmth eased in grasping it grew
its fullness turning uncomfortable
                                      unwieldy it released what was too much
And in this way of gather and loss
                                      the bowl in this mountain came to be
like a long marriage scoured by change
                                      by avalanche and melt
the daily orbital spin
                                      What remains is studded with granite
debris   leftover loaves   massive ideas
                                      holds of cold cleft and caved
a rock-riddled sink
                                      grizzled with pine and whisk of spruce
softened by birch leaf-sulk
                                      seasoned ferment of sun and root
Crack the bowl
                                      and water like light fills the crazed surface
supplants the matter
                          the must of mushrooms   moss in crevice and till
Today the deer-crossed moose haunt
                                        lies silent and barren except for
the snow a glistening
                                        robe descending slow
See how it buries our skis my love
                                        our slender paltry trails

Moon Bird Tree

The worm moon is super
this spring falling on equinox
it wakes me from a dream where

I'm in a car – my son driving –
we try to maneuver our way
out of a parking lot full of icy
snow banks lit by our headlights

he guns the engine we go forward
to go backward to get turned around
like worms readying to mend themselves
into what they were meant to be

~

Jung calls the process of transformation
individuation the personal and the collective
cobbled into one whole being and I

believe I believe in it as I walk
this morning along the river
by the boathouse a passel of

sailboats newly unwrapped
for their spring launch and
I spy on the edge of the dock

the goose who would be me
it gazes down mesmerized
by the ripples as the river talks

to the sun   but the cormorants –
my familiars – slip under the surface
then reappear   anonymous

~

The birch –
the second tree cut this week
on my path to school –

 had kept on for months after
getting *X*'d in neon orange for the saw
its bark erupting into a thousand
yellow hooded caps

 the woody fungi marching
to the very top of the tree
like Tashtego on the mast
going down with the Pequod

 and I must remember
(hold inside) all of this

The day my father died

  I went to the Armory
Center for the Arts
and learned to make
a   mandala out of
 sand
        Spring was
converting   too
the   whole ground
growing soft with
what was
 coming

        A mandala
made of elements that vary
and elements that repeat
guides the eye   inward
 and out again
         In   this
universe   lines asseverate
symmetry and
  balance
         in-between-
spaces   wait   to be filled with
color   the full meaning to
emerge as one   hue   is
laid down beside
 another

           I surrendered
to the material   reached
for red the first color
to fall off the
 spectrum
          camouflage for
creatures in the
 deep-sea
               surely   red
 is the color   death   would
convert into   if it were not
  black   or white

            The sand
was fine as salt pinched between
  finger and thumb
               there was
a pattern   for grief   I tried to
find it   on the square
 of paper
           Rainbows
of sand grains grew   unwieldy
small dunes unmanageable
 art

    My father's life of days
and minutes ended hours ago
within this   day of hours   in
  my   life

                    I   tried
the yellow and   the green
and   the blue   each
had something
 to offer

                    It   should
have been beautiful   but the
boundaries grew   muddy and
varicose   what I tried to fix
I smudged
            a makeshift
 map this letting go

Demolition of the Old Hotel

A firehose plays relentlessly
fiddles the billow of dust
blossom of debris
and I cannot
turn away
        the stream
of pedestrians flows past
as I watch what always
in my time was standing
now coming to
unbe
     pink pillows untuck
from caving beams and sinews
detach as the pulverizer
crumples story into story –
all tossed into the swallowing
hauler
     a grappler dismantles
inner rooms and floors hang
down like straggly bangs
one bone-white strut
wobbles caught
in cabling web
        gutted I feel
unwalled bricks fall two by
three loose teeth my tongue
glides across my own   unroofed
the maw of this hotel gapes
to daylight

       something in there
must recall how it was like this
once before – a morning's light
finding new walls new infant self
and the many hands that brought
it forth
    slap of trowel mortar
drywall strokes of color-sopped
brushes primer pigment
eggshell finish –
        what will they find
when finally they clear this plot?
Remnants of conversations
kisses A beginning?
        Is it possible
to remember how it was
and what built this edifice
nick by nick knocked entire
falling now! *down*

The year is new again

  but all those who've left
will still be gone what is
the use of all this new

  the weight of the dead
on my heels as I go
forward drawing nearer

The Sacred

You run like a herd of luminous deer
and I am dark, I am forest.

                    Rainer Maria Rilke, *Book of Hours*

Prefigure

What trick of light lays the city out
flat against March's blue baize?
Seams of cars glint above a terrazzo
of old ice. Gaunt trees pin the verge.

Skyline in silhouette denies entry.
The pocked and mottled grey river holds
sun's glare steady in its silvery raw silk,
says, *Look at me, Don't look at me.*

I imagine slipping into the skirt of ice
its lace of gulls and geese, hem of trash.
Surely fishes flash and stir below in wait
of spring, its predators, its promises.

Theory of Everything

I walk the shadow
of the railing
        it is straight
and keeps me close
to the river
        though it moves
throughout the day as earth
turns   it is a steady shadow
to guide my feet
        as I ponder
the emptiness from which
everything comes and
to which all
returns

      Gogol wrote himself
into a place of incompatibility
with the evil of the
world
      To be good
    is to be gone
           his own family
owned serfs and dead souls

he imagined redemption
wrote it down
        then burned
those chapters   quit eating

and died
> his Overcoat
>> remains

> I want a theory
of everything   a theory that begins
in one place and connects
to another
> like this river
below me that divides cities
even as it unites
and sustains

> I want a self-evident truth
something I can show my mother
I want to say love of *this*
cannot abide love
of *that*

> I glance up
and catch the lit two-thirds
of the day moon
> its faint
reflected light holds fast
in the cold spring sky

Spring, and

    free of ice
    the river
    ribbed this
    yellow day
    by sculler
    oar steady
    dip *Stroke!*
Stroke! Ready
at the catch!
   Oh bury
   the blade
   and bury
    it again
     Revel
in the wake –

Spring upspring

    of wild and ferment *rumspringa*
all together letting go of exactness of meet and
right of should and should and should *Yes*
to effervescence   to the fizz of earthy-watery
kapha dosha *Run* we run   with the millions
of   fresh-born   through the warming   dirt
we run   like calves   in   bluestem   pastures
immeasurable host   fecund fields of wildrye
switchgrass paintbrush cone-flower   sage
the   holy   wild   prairie   calls us home
to feast   on   green the green that   only
fire   after   winter   can   bring

There is only the sacred and the desecrated
— *Francis of Assisi*

My cat's expression of holy –
Me she says bumping my chin
chewing on my pencil

      the rain too   is
      air   multiplied

    o

The hardware store our destination
I step off the curb with
my dog Dover

      the street is empty
the way streets in dreams
are empty   what I see
is what I'm looking for

      the door we'll enter
waits on the other side of the strangely
lacquered pavement –
        trick of the light
that orangey-yellow-greenish glow
before a storm

                then I spot
a line of metal barricades the reason
no cars
         and a Wolf comes loping
toward us its grey and white coat glossy
in the mystical light
              It wants Dover!
Help I say as if to myself *Help*

      A man looks up
his blond dog pees on the grass
and I can see he has no idea

        All I can do is wake

    o

Francis what gave you this idea?
Was it the birds their wings of light
and perfect oval eggs the flesh on the foot
of a newborn child   the first holy
leaves of anything green   earth's cathedral
of pumice and lapis rent-free sanctity
you begin Francis   then you
begin again a lease on new

    o

The Ukrainian artist was seventy years old
the first time she held a brush

  her son banished to a penal colony
  her husband and daughter buried

    I will paint my future she said
    I will give it bird and flower

  blues and yellows   my green
future in a sacred embrace of these walls

    o concrete surface take hold of my dream
    bring it into vine give it window and desk

let what is me be garden
    live here o feathered song

      Paint it Feed it
    and I shall open in time

    o

Two sisters –
    when one spoke pearls fell from her mouth
      and the other frogs and toads

and me Sister Three (each sister in me)
      in my ears pearls and toads

        amphibious wisdom I
         take to the road

  o

Bonaventure gave us Francis *clean*
Francis *beloved* Who does not need
  an apologist and confessor?
  a translator of peripatetic intent

someone who sees us
as their vested interest

        their very lively lovelihood
         (*Be my bon adventure!*)

  o

  Say I start right now
paint my house   my inner vessel
with a new teaching –

  a new Francis
whatever *contuition*
is required to see
  the rivulets of holiness
      in cloudberry and leaf

    in blue spider veins
and ripening tomato –

to tread the holy path of talking stones
beneath a Sister Moon God's very son a sheep!

    (but Francis must I empty my freezer
        decouple my household from meat?)

how personal
need an ethic be?

    the exact change

  (exact change only)

      o

Dear Frances did you wonder how
the human skin detects temperature?

      Your answer is an answer
to everything

    you shed your father's silks
for sackcloth that rasped against your skin
    gathering in its roughened flax
      the feathers and fur
    of your new wild friends

     denying self you cured all you touched –

even the water that washed your feet
came away holy
             releasing the fevers
                of cows and lambs

        o

I, branched dowsing rod, seek You
Holiness, to be my find

  O hidden Stream of goodness
call to my diviner, draw on that
in me which rhymes with You

May I sense what I cannot see
persistent and sure as my cat

May we meet as in a state of
before: You coursing under-
ground and me believing

        o

        the refusal
of comfort is comfort

the callous of love does not
    admit bitterness

      o

When I teach about the language
 of intimacy and power

    I teach the words
   that insulate the stark
     request:

  would you mind
would it be okay with you if –

and I consider the chickadee
the *chick a dee-dee-dee-dee*–
each *dee* a measure of urgency

  a thermometer of sound

      o

Once in the White Mountains
on the Greeley Pond trail I stopped
by a pine tree near the parking lot
and the chorus of *chick-a-dee-dee-dee*

grew bright and bold one bird
nearest me its throat pulsing with song
called everyone to come the air flocked
alive chickadees primed for a handout
and I didn't know this learning they had
and to never go to the pond without
a handful of seeds these birds of Francis
sought Francis in me!

    o

Francis, you're a mattress
against the bullet

    Wake up!
The rich are using you

    o

What doesn't begin as an irritation?
an unendurable itch – an expulsion
and accommodation the annoying
undeniable new with no vision of
what's to come

    The Bang begat Elephants and
Sycamores and Shakespeare who knows
what from where

      I inhale pearly nights and mornings
and hold the argument in my iridescent sheen
          pure making-do I am

    o

O grand Machine built to blunder and
bluster
      feel the inside coil of muscle
and rivering blood
          listen up Heart you
four-chambered ear
        hear the little quartet
of Harmony and beat

     the homogenitor of synching
     pulses raises the ante
     the individual humanoid
     has such thin boundary

    yet in you little Body
the march of molecules
   the small insistent Spirit breathes
               its mandate
   the inexorable Animation shared
with all that lives!

　　　　Say to the bristly Jay in the Spruce
bullying its neighbor Squirrel –

　　　*I-Jay   I-Spruce   I-Squirrel
　　　　I-Keep-of-Flame!*

　　　(*for now* says the intumescent eye   the swollen
and diseased   the desecrated I)

　　　　o

it was Francis' eyes that did him in
they wept and crusted and pained
him to no end   thick-scabbed sick
eyes buckled lids lashes sucked in
and under   scraping his cornea thin
scarring opacity   vision turned
inward
　　Hello Brother Fire! he said
to the flame recruited to cauterize
the wounds of his eyes

　　　　someone held the fire
　　　　　　as Francis sang
someone
had to leave the room

　　　　Prayer – his surgeon
　　his staff his supper his succor –

till perfectly he saw the six-winged
angel on the cross and welcomed
the gift of the five stigmata
calling *Lord my Refuge*
and my Portion in the land
of the living

      o

What astronauts saw they tried out new
language to tell us   So too the almost-died
That beautiful awful Edge once peered
endears the Pilgrim to the original land
the living wild knowable land

Granted a new liver a drinker
rarely returns to drink

        Such are the gifts of Extremity

      What in me might be revived?
Someone please lend me an Eye

      o

The child in my dream was full
of judgment   Certain in her
pronouncement   the blue-eyed

girl   repeated what she'd heard
evil this and *evil* that poor parrot
ripe for light (could she be me?)

      o

in the everlasting unremitting undertow of expansion
              we grows thin
        an ache of connection

      o

I can tell you how the end happens
says the toad it's preceded by
a nor'easter bearing a deluge
wind rain terrible noise and you
huddle close family neighbors
you feel the dread barely contained
within your clustered shivering bodies
    then the dam gives way and
your home dissolves in the night
morning before you realize truly
the end has come the life
you'd known – impossible

      o

The heron stabs a circle
   of sun shedding river
      – flash of foil! –

     then swallows the wriggling
light whole

      the heron's long graceful
    neck disfigured now
       with a bulging knob
          stretches up and out
     to make room
    in its pulsating throat
  for the sharp-edged coin

  what's been swallowed
resists the final requirement
    does not slip
   into its conclusion
but grips the confining
walls and bends their frame

     fins tail thrash
 writhe the entire self
beleaguered engages
in the search for its ease
of river

      the heron answers
with a beakful of water

    then wades through
      clacking reeds   pauses
        to salute the sky
          extending its gullet
            one final gulp
          and elegance returns
        to its silhouette

    o

each Rose new again
in each season the same
branch the same root
the same plot of soil
offers *Another*
and *Another*

the perfect is a circle
God says this every day

Song

    The morning breeze
       has no plan for beauty

    the river does not say to the sun
       Stroke my ruffled back

        the arch of the bridge does not insist
on its glittering ornament of light & shadow

the feathers on the mallard's head
    express only numinous greens

      & the *I* grows quiet
    (except for the song)

Notes and Acknowledgments

The dedication page contains quotes from Fanny Howe's book, *Manimal Woe,* Arrowsmith Press, 2021.

The verses at the beginning of each section come from *Rilke's Book of Hours: Love Poems to God,* translated by Anita Barrows and Joanna Macy, Penguin Books, 1997.

The title, "uttering joyous leaves all its life," is from Walt Whitman's poem "I saw in Louisiana a live-oak growing," about a lone live oak that flourished despite its loneliness.

"Unbound" contains a line from "Crossing Brooklyn Ferry" by Walt Whitman; Fanny Longfellow's mourning brooch is archived at the Longfellow House-Washington's Headquarters National Historic Site in Cambridge, Massachusetts.

"The engines keep playing here" refers to St. Catherine, a Christian saint and martyr; the Wheel of Catherine, an instrument of torture commonly used in Europe from antiquity through the early modern period, was said to have shattered at the martyr's touch so she was ordered to be beheaded instead.

The title, "bare ruin'd choirs," is a line from Shakespeare's Sonnet #73.

The epigraph in "When the Border Patrol Agent Sleeps" is a quote from Terence Shiggs, a veteran border patrol agent in Texas; the story aired on National Public Radio on June 23, 2018: npr.org/2018/06/23/622885413/family-separations-is-not-new-the-scale-of-it-is-border-patrol-veteran-says.

Edip Cansever (August 8, 1928 – May 28, 1986) was a Turkish poet influenced by French surrealism; my friend Adnan Adam Onart and I worked together on translations of several of his poems.

"Moon Bird Tree" refers to Carl Jung's theory of individuation; Jung wrote that "the aim of individuation is nothing less than to divest the self of the false wrappings of the persona, on the one hand, and the suggestive power of primordial images on the other" (1977), *The Relations Between the Ego and the Unconscious. Collected Works*, Routledge & Kegan Paul. In this poem, there is also a reference to Melville's *Moby Dick*, with the mention of Tashtego, a Native American harpooneer who dies clinging to the mast as the Pequod sinks.

The title, "Now when darkness starts in midafternoon", is a line from Eavan Boland's poem, "How We Were Transfigured."

In the sequence, "There is only the sacred and the desecrated," details from the life of St. Francis of Assisi are taken from an article by Joan Acocella, titled "Rich Man, Poor Man," in *The New Yorker* (2013). Included in that article is a quote from a Marxist critic who called St. Francis a "mattress to the bullet" and said the rich were using the Franciscan Friars.

The artist who took up her brush when she was seventy years old is Raika Polina from Ukraine; more information and images of her extraordinary work can be found here: naive.in.ua/en/author/raiko-polina/.

In 2021, during the pandemic, U.S.-based scientists David Julius and Ardem Patapoutian were awarded the Nobel Prize in physiology or medicine for their discoveries of receptors that allow humans to feel temperature and touch.

Grateful acknowledgment is due to the editors of the following publications in which these poems, some in earlier versions, first appeared:

"Parable of the Moss Piglet," *AGNI;* "The year is new again," *Bagel Bard Anthology #14;* "Spring, and," *Boston Globe;* "Spring upspring," *Club Plum;* "Moon Bird Tree," *Constellations;* "Unbound," *Funicular Magazine*; "To the raven feeding on carrion on the side of the road," "Translating Edip Cansever's poem with my friend Adnan Onart," *Gargoyle;* "Prefigure," *House Mountain Review;* "Germination," *Humana Obscura;* "On my way to work," "The Border Patrol Agent" [as "When The Border Patrol Agent Sleeps"], "The first story of the snow," "Song," *Ibbetson Street;* "Harold calls to me," *Interim;* "Birth of Night," *JuxtaProse;* "In the bin of what I'm looking for," *Kithe;* "Sometimes Necessity," "uttering joyous leaves all its life" [as "After Whitman's, "I saw in Louisiana a live-oak growing""], "There is only the sacred and the desecrated," *Lily Poetry Review;* "Once a molecule said," *Meat for Tea;* "Waiting," *Minute Magazine;* "Lodged beside my left ventricle a little village on a blue volcano ringed with red clay paths," "What the trees see to," *Maine Review;* "At the cemetery," *Mojave River Review;* "In the company of grief," *New Plains Review;* "Canoeing at Dusk" [as "Dusk on Diamond Pond"], *On and Off the Road: Poems of New Hampshire;* "How readily I assign holy," *Pangyrus;* "The interview," *Plume;* "Bare ruin'd choirs –," "In the Park" [as "What makes *place*"], "The day my father died," "Demolition of the Old Hotel," *Poetry Porch;* "The engines keep playing here," "A Broken Sonnet for the Sparrow Trapped in the Interfaith Center on the 3rd Floor of the McCormick Building at UMass Boston Overlooking the Harbor," *Presence: A Journal of Catholic Poetry;* "Theory of Everything," *Psaltery & Lyre;* "you can read it in its rings," *Revolute;* "Late October Leaves," *Rust + Moth;* "Parable of the Krill," *Sutterville Review;* "Now when darkness starts in mid-afternoon," *The Worcester Review;* "from the world of things a feeling," *Wend.*

Pushcart Nominations: "The first story of the snow," "When The Border Patrol Agent Sleeps," "Once a molecule said," "A Broken Sonnet for the Sparrow Trapped in the Interfaith Center on the 3rd Floor of the McCormick Building at UMass Boston Overlooking the Harbor"

Beals Poetry Prize (finalist): "Lincoln's Throat"

Sidewalk Poetry Installation in Cambridge, Massachusetts: "Spring, and"

This work is dedicated, with gratitude, to the memory of Fanny Howe, Danielle Legros Georges, Ellin Sarot, Charles Coe, Neil Silberblatt, Jennifer Martelli; how could you all leave in the span of one terrible year?

Thank you to Bruce Weigl and the Thursday morning poets, to the poets in the New England Poetry Club workshop, and in Bert Stern and Tam Neville's workshop.

Thanks to Eileen Myles, Jenny Barber, and Lloyd Schwartz for writing the blurbs, and to Michael McInnis for the book design. Once again, I'm indebted to poet, friend, and editor Eileen Cleary for your vision and fortitude.

Ever grateful to Linda Haviland Conte for your friendship and encouragement. My profound thanks to Hilary Sallick for reading my poetry with your whole heart, and for sensing the structure of this manuscript.

Love always to Steve and our sons, Liam and Kai (special thanks for your cover art!), and to our family companions, Dunya, Dover, and the dearly missed, inimitable Coulier.

Author Bio

Mary Buchinger is the author of eight collections of poetry; in addition to *There Is Only the Sacred and the Desecrated* (Lily Poetry Review Books, 2026; Paul Nemser Book Prize, Honorable Mention), recent books include *The Book of Shores* (Lily Poetry Review Books, 2024; Permafrost Book Prize in Poetry finalist; Hillary Gravendyk Prize, semifinalist), *Navigating the Reach* (Salmon Poetry, Honors, 2024 Massachusetts Book Award), and *Virology* (Lily Poetry Review Books, 2022), and she is the winner of the 2024 Elyse Wolf/Slate Roof Chapbook Prize. Her poetry has appeared in many journals, including *AGNI, Pedestal Magazine, Plume, Salt Hill, Salamander, Seneca Review*, and is permanently installed in Cambridge, where she lives and served as Poetry Ambassador. She was a Peace Corps Volunteer in Ecuador and earned a doctorate in linguistics from Boston University; she teaches at the Massachusetts College of Pharmacy and Health Sciences. Website: MaryBuchinger.com

www.ingramcontent.com/pod-product-compliance
Lightning Source LLC
LaVergne TN
LVHW040108080526
838202LV00045B/3816